The Immigrant
on Columbus Way

The Immigrant
on Columbus Way

*Notes on Early Life in America
and Citizenship*

Deba Uwadiae

To order additional copies of this book, contact:
Xlibris
1-888-795-4274
www.Xlibris.com
Orders@Xlibris.com
545690

CONTENTS

Dedicated to all immigrants,
from the beginning

Chapter 1

Arrive USA

Tuesday June 7, 2011

The Turkish Airways airbus A340 aircraft from Istanbul, Turkey touched down on the runway of the Chicago O'Hare International Airport, Illinois, United States of America at about 3pm ending an almost 24hours of a journey that traversed three continents—Africa, Europe and America.

It was a smooth touchdown on a level runway.

The journey started Monday June 6, 2011 at 7pm from a quiet and dark, Bashiru Owe Street, Ikeja, Lagos, Nigeria in West Africa. The less than 300meters-long or about 328yards dusty stretch of a street is usually a highly populated market place during the day as it has one computer college and a college of technology, housed in three different five-floor buildings, owned by the same person; one elementary school located in two three-bedroom flats in two opposite buildings; several computer accessories' shops and offices of various professions. No wonder that area of Ikeja is called Computer Village!

There is always no space to park a car as at from 7am and the crowd of students, workers, buyers and sellers is always a chaos every day, except Sunday.

But when night comes, the street becomes deserted and virtually 'dead' especially when there is no electricity which has become normal many years ago.

As the plane taxied to one of the gates at Terminal 5, the excitement of the family of five, a couple and three children, was palpable. The processing of immigrating to the United States of America which started with the playing of the US Visa lottery on the last day of the exercise in 2010 had seemed a long wait but the culmination of aircraft touching down safely on the soil of the United States of America wiped out the seemingly anxiety in the long wait.

We looked through the aircraft windows as the speed of the aircraft reduced getting close to one of the gates in 'a stop and move' fashion and finally it came to a stop. We could feel all the bumps and knocks on the aircraft as the gangway was being pushed close to the front door and as the undercarriage was being secured for safety.

Our two teenage children, Uyi (15) and Abi (14) were the first to, excitedly, step out of the aircraft into the gangway passage with their backpacks strapped to their left shoulders. My wife, Tolu, second daughter, Eki (9), and myself followed as three security men with their dogs positioned themselves at the end of the passage into the hall way with their dogs sniffing away the hand-held luggage of every passenger.

We walked the long hall way to the immigration check. It was a long and winding walk of about 20minutes. There were already spiraling lines of multitude of visitors. Our line dragged for over 40minutes before it got to our turn.

"Hallo!" a very friendly and welcoming immigration officer collected our passports and the large white parcel we brought along from the American Embassy in Lagos, Nigeria with an instruction that it should only be opened by the immigration officers at the point—of-entry airport, being one of the documents of immigrants on the Diversity Visa Program 2010 (US Visa lottery).

The diversity visa program "is unofficially known as the green card lottery system and individuals from around the world can apply for a U.S. Permanent Resident Card. The program will give foreign residents an opportunity to live and work in the U.S. Each year, the U.S. Department of State opens registration in October and applicants have the chance to fill out forms online until early November.

The Diversity Visa program is administered annually by the State Department under the Immigration and Nationality Act of 1990.

While the application is open to the residents around the world, the program is specifically aimed at attracting those who meet eligibility requirements and are from countries with historically low immigration rates.

To be eligible for DV consideration, an applicant must have a minimum of a high school education and have worked for at least two years in the past five years. Additionally, the applicant must have gone through a minimum of two years' of training in his or her field." (Immigration Direct)

About 50,000 visas are issued annually on the Diversity Immigrant Visa Program and the first program was DV-1995.

The immigration officer treated one passport after the other beginning with Tolu, who is the principal, (she entered for the visa lottery) and administered the swearing of oath. When he got to our that-day-14years' old daughter, Abi he said "Happy Birthday! You are 14 today! Incidentally, that is the age she is entitled by law to swear to an oath like the three of you," referring to Tolu, Uyi and me.

Not to say the least that Abi was very excited participating in the swearing to an oath which she could not do at the Embassy in Lagos during the visa interview as she was 13years and 10months at the time.

"The passports will serve as documents such as the green card for whatever documentation you may need to carry out pending when the green cards are sent to your contact address," he informed us as he handed over all the passports and now-opened parcel to us.

The parcel contained the medical reports from the medical examination we did before the interview.

He then directed us to another point where further immigrants' documentation is done. It took us about two minutes to walk to the area.

There were already seated in the rows of seats a couple, a woman with her three daughters, they traveled from Lagos with us, and a man waiting to process their own documents when we got to the area. We handed over our passports and other papers as directed by the immigration officer that checked us in and as demanded by the officer who was happy to receive us. He ushered us into the seats opposite the counter.

The processing took about 30minutes as our restless nine year old daughter, Eki kept moving from one seat to the other looking forward to seeing the 'real inside' of America through the Chicago prism.

We went for our baggage, already gathered on the ground beside the conveyer, and being surreptitiously watched from the exit gates by the customs and security officers. We put them onto three airport trollies and headed for the the exit.

As we stepped outside the automatic glass door of the Chicago O'Hare International Airport into the bright sunny day of Tuesday June 7, 2011 it was as if the air, the cars and buses dropping off and picking up airport guests were, in concerted agreement, welcoming the five of us, immigrants from Nigeria, Africa into the land of the United States of America and chorusing: "Welcome to the United States of America!"

An African-American lady overseeing the yellow-painted airport cabs lined up to our left beckoned to us.

"You need a taxi?" she asked.

I went to her to inquire how to get to Greyhound Bus station in Chicago. We had been told to take the Greyhound bus to Columbus, Ohio.

"It is between $25 and $30 depending on the traffic," she said.

That is because the cabs carry fare meters that work efficiently to the joy of the operators when traffic is heavy. More is charged if the traffic is heavy and movement is annoyingly slow.

The lady got a bigger vehicle for a family of five—a mini-van—and we loaded our six boxes into the van trunk.

The van headed south east of the airport, turning left into the interstate I-190 east freeway.

It journeyed into the high rise buildings lining up, on both sides, the Kennedy Expressway in the 5.4 miles distance to the bus station.

A huge colorful billboard to our right towering above the freeway, of Nigerian—born Israel Idonijie, then of the Chicago Bears, was the most encouraging experience one would want to have on a day, coming for the first time, into the United States of America from Nigeria.

His big image on the billboard with a smiling face was a compelling assurance that is filled with a kind of deep insight and meaning beyond description, but like saying, "Welcome brothers, you've all come to the right place, the United States of America!"

The van exited 79A for Cumberland Avenue S/IL-171 S. It merged onto IL-171 S/N Cumberland Avenue, turning right onto W Bryn Mawr Avenue and taking the first right onto N Delphia Avenue. It made a U-turn almost immediately and took the first left onto W Bryn Mawr Avenue.

At this point anxiety set in because we have lost count of turnings. It was becoming one turn and another turn as if there was not going to be an end to the journey. But that is what it is as we later learned about journeying in metropolitan cities, like Chicago, in the United States of America. Some roads are strictly one-way in order to manage the free flow of traffic and so getting to certain parts of the cities, especially in the downtown area, will require going round and round, if possible.

The van continued to IL-171 N/N Cumberland Avenue after a turn to the left off W Bryn Mawr Avenue. It took the first left and from the van we could see the sign post outside the station—Greyhound Lines 5800 North Cumberland Avenue, Chicago. We got to the bus station accumulating so much time and our fare was $40, quite beyond what the lady at the airport estimated.

Time of arrival at the bus station was around 6.20pm.

It was another journey within the bus station. I went to the only window opened at the ticketing counter. Ticket to Columbus, Ohio cost $48 for an adult and $28 for a child—four of us adults and one child. Unfortunately for us, the bus will not be leaving the station until 11.10pm. Our ticket purchased time was 6.54pm, meaning a waiting time of almost five hours to departure. It was not expected! We had thought we will have a bus waiting and ready to leave for Columbus instantly.

Tickets could have been cheaper if we had bought it ahead. We were charged separately for the six boxes and so paid almost $400 altogether for the trip.

Our departure was announced at 11pm and those of us traveling to and towards the direction of Columbus, Ohio marched to the bus and lined up at the entrance for our tickets to be checked by the bus driver for boarding. Not too many people in the bus as thought and so we got some good, convenient and comfortable positions to journey through the night; sleep and hope to wake up at destination before 8.10am our expected time of arrival in Columbus on Wednesday June 8.

Chapter 2

Journey to Columbus

Wednesday June 8

"Why Columbus?" A question always being asked whenever I introduce myself as a new immigrant that his first place of abode in the United States is Columbus, Ohio. Our hosts, Michael Akinrinade and his family, encouraged us to come to Columbus, Ohio when we informed them of our desire to register them as the family we intend staying with pending our settling down in the United States. It is one of the requests in the Visa Lottery/ diversity immigrants' form.

"Columbus is a beautiful place to raise the kids," Debra, Micheal's wife had told us.

"**Columbus** is the capital of and the largest city in the U.S. state of Ohio. The Columbus metropolitan statistical area (MSA), which encompasses several counties, is the third largest in Ohio, after the Cleveland MSA and the Cincinnati MSA (which includes portions of Kentucky and Indiana). Columbus is the 15th largest city in the United States of America. It is the county seat of Franklin County, yet the city has expanded and annexed portions of adjoining Delaware County and Fairfield County.

Named for explorer Christopher Columbus, the city was founded in 1812 at the confluence of the Scioto and Olentangy rivers, and assumed the functions of state capital in 1816.

The population of the city was 787,033 at the 2010 census, making it the most populous city in Ohio. Although Columbus was the 15th largest city in the United States, its metropolitan area was 28th largest, with 2,308,509 residents. It is the fourth most populous state capital in the United States.

According to the U.S. Census Bureau, the Columbus Combined Statistical Area (which also includes Marion and Chillicothe) has a population of 2,348,495.

The city has a diverse economy based on education, government, insurance, banking, fashion, defense, aviation, food, clothes, logistics, steel, energy, medical research, health care, hospitality, retail, and technology.

Columbus is home to the world's largest private research and development foundation, the Battelle Memorial Institute; Chemical Abstracts Service, the world's largest clearinghouse of chemical information; Netjets, the world's largest fractional ownership jet aircraft fleet; and The Ohio State University, the nation's largest campus.

As of 2013, the city has the headquarters of four corporations in the U.S. Fortune 500, including Nationwide Mutual Insurance Company, American Electric Power; Big Lots; Cardinal Health and Wendy's corporations are also based in the Columbus metropolitan area. Major foreign corporations operating or with divisions in the city include Germany-based Siemens and Roxane Laboratories, Finland-based Vaisala, Tomasco Mulciber Inc., A Y Manufacturing, Yachiyo of America and US Yachiyo, Inc." (Wikipidia, the free encyclopedia)

Michael, our host, was already at the Greyhound bus station on 111 E Town Street, Columbus, Ohio at about 8.45am when our bus arrived. We climbed down from the bus and to the luggage compartment where we pulled down our boxes as supervised by the bus driver.

We dragged the boxes along into the terminal building and Michael was gladly there to welcome us. He led the way towards the exit. His silver colored Honda Odyssey mini-van, glittering under the summer morning sun, was parked close to the entrance of the station, some yards away from the road with several mounted car park coin machines standing on a row as if in a guard of honors for the new immigrants.

We lifted our boxes into the opened trunk of the van under an unusual watchful and intimidating gaze, though harmless, of the gigantic 11-floors building Holiday Inn opposite the Greyhound bus station in the downtown Columbus.

Michael drove straight ahead into the quiet and seemingly empty road at about 9am until we got to a ramp on the right which merged onto I-71 N freeway.

The streets were virtually empty at that time of the morning and we were curious whether workers were yet to resume work.

"It is a quiet city. Far different from Lagos," Michael explained.

I had an image of a city like London, United Kingdom or Lagos, Nigeria and probably New York where hundreds of people at that time of the morning, in similar commercial center, will be seen hurriedly moving in different directions with heavy traffic on the roads. That is not Columbus, Ohio. People walking on the streets that morning could easily be counted on the finger tips and the vehicles driving past as well. The city seemed to be deliberately planned that way. But not the interstate I-71N where lots of vehicles are seen at the time that morning all going at between the speed minimum of 65miles and maximum of 75miles per hour. Some leaving the freeway at the different exits while others continuing their journey.

Our destination being Omega Drive, off Cleveland Avenue, we exited through Exit 116 on the I-71 N freeway into Morse Road turning to the right. There are about six traffic lights of little over 340feet distance between each of them on the 2.3miles to Cleveland Avenue junction where we made a turn to the left.

As we drove along Morse Road towards Cleveland Avenue, we heard an emergency siren and a police van was driving in the opposite direction. Every vehicle, even those already passed by the traffic light, came to a stop on both sides of the road so that the police van could move without any hindrance. Almost following the police car behind were a red-colored fire brigade truck and an ambulance. All vehicles remained at complete stop giving the emergency vehicles enough room to maneuver. We continued our journey after the emergency vehicles had passed just like other vehicles on the road.

Between the Cleveland Avenue junction on Morse Road/Morse Crossing to Wallcrest Boulevard junction on the 35miles speed limit road are two traffic lights. The Google map search, is our only source of destination, estimated the distance to be a 3-minute drive and 0.7miles.

We have come to see Columbus as a city that does not compromise effective and efficient traffic and road management. It is such an example of implementation of an ideal traffic and road management!

At about 9.20am June 8, 2011 our journey which started from Lagos, Nigeria at about 7pm on June 6 terminated at Omega Drive, Columbus, Ohio, United States of America.

Debra, Micheal's wife and their two sons, Damola and Debola were already waiting.

"Welcome!" they all chorused as the car doors opened outside the garage.

It's welcome to the United States of America, our new home.

Chapter 3

Social Security Number

Thursday June 9

I had always wondered how important is the Social Security Card before coming to the United States of America. It is very important! We do not use it at all in my country, Nigeria. But almost 24hours in Columbus, Ohio at about 8.05am, we were on our way from Omega Drive to the United States Social Security Administration office at 1051 Worthington Woods Boulevard, Columbus. It is an estimated 17-minute drive. We drove out that morning savoring the sunny and warm weather and the rows of buildings on both sides of Wallcrest Boulevard, making a right turn onto Cleveland Avenue.

Few minutes along Cleveland Avenue to our left is the Meijer mega-store before the 161/Dublin Grandville Road. And adjacent it is Family Dollar on a stretch of stores that also includes the Post Office. As we continued on our journey, crossing the Schrock Road junction, where you have the CVS Pharmaceutical Store, we could see the Mount Carmel Hospital to our right and adjacent to the hospital is the entrance leading to one of JP Morgan Chase campuses in Columbus.

We turned left onto W Main Street which continued, same direction, after 3minutes into Worthington Boulevard. The destination, 1051 Worthington Woods Boulevard is Worthington Business Center, on the left.

We were there before the doors opened to customers and some few people were outside the building, waiting as well. At 9am, the doors were opened and we went in, picked our numbers on the line and took our seats towards the back of the rows of seats because of space.

Our position on the line was number 7. The number '7' has become very unique to us as a family. We went for our Immigration Visa interview on April 7, 2011; we were number 7 on the line for our immigrant interview at the US Embassy in Lagos and got June 7, 2011 as our departure date from Lagos, Nigeria to Chicago, USA on the Turkish Airlines.

The Social Security number is one of the requirements for getting a job, starting a school, at hospitals, when opening a bank account, applying for state identity card or driver license and some other benefits.

According to the US Social Security Administration, "You need a Social Security number to get a job, collect Social Security benefits and receive some other government services. But you don't often need to show your Social Security card. Do not carry your card with you. Keep it in a safe place with your other important papers."

Important is that "All documents submitted must be either originals or copies certified by the issuing agency. We cannot accept photocopies or notarized copies of documents."

The card is for adult and child. It is for US Citizen, foreign born US Citizen and Non citizen.

However, "In general, only non citizens who have permission to work from the Department of Homeland Security (DHS) can apply for a Social Security number." If you do not have permission to work but need a Social Security number for other purposes, see "If you do not have permission to work" for further information" on the website.

It added that, "To prove your U.S. immigration status, you must show your current U.S. immigration document, such as Form I-551 (Lawful Permanent Resident Card, Machine Readable Immigrant Visa), I-766 (work permit) or I-94 (Arrival/Departure Record). If you are an F-1 or M-1 student, you also must show your I-20, Certificate of Eligibility for Non immigrant Student Status. If you are a J-1 or J-2 exchange visitor, you must show your DS-2019, Certificate of Eligibility for Exchange Visitor Status."

The Social Security Administration handles other areas like Retirement, Disability claims, Survivor benefits, Supplemental Security Income, Medicare benefits, and Business Services. It delivers 'services through a nationwide network of over 1,400 offices that include regional offices, field offices, card centers, teleservice centers, processing centers, hearing offices, the Appeals Council, and our State and territorial partners, the Disability Determination Services. We also have a presence in U.S. embassies around the globe. For the public, we are the "face of the government." The rich diversity of our employees mirrors the public we serve.'

There are two customer desks at the Worthington Boulevard office of the Social Security Administration in Columbus, Ohio. Our turn came and we were in the second window where a female official attended to us. We handed over our documents including passports to her. Forms were filled for the five of us. Names, birthdays, and addresses must correspond with what are in passports and other documents.

It took us about 20minutes to complete our documentation. The female official informed us that it will take about 14 working days for our social security numbers to be out. Though, some people are said to have received theirs within seven working days. The first letter from the Social Security Administration office arrived to our box on Tuesday June 21, being 12days after the application. It was dated June 17 and informed us that our applications were being processed.

The first batch of social security cards, for Tolu, Uyi and I, was delivered on Friday June 24, being 15days after the application. One of our daughters got hers Tuesday June 28, that is 19days after the application. We learned through those who had experience that it is normal for the one of the family's cards to be delayed for security reasons and so we waited a while for the last card to come.

When it was becoming too long, I called the Social Security Administration office on Thursday July 14 asking for our delayed number/card. It was received on Wednesday July 20, thus completing the receipt of Social Security Number by the five of us. It took 41days for the last person in the family to get the SSN.

We learned that some people get it earlier and perhaps others get it far beyond.

With the arrival of all the social security numbers we were good to go!

The implication of not having the Social Security Number is that benefits associated with having it, such as getting job, school, driver license, state identity card and state medical service cannot be obtained until the number is available.

Therefore, we had to wait for the SSN to start processing some of these necessities.

At every point of documentation for these necessities we are requested to provide our Resident Permit and the Social Security Number.

The information on the passports served as the resident permit until our Green Cards were delivered to us on Thursday August 11, 2011—65days after arriving the United States through the Chicago O'Hare International Airport, Illinois.

Chapter 4

Driver License

Monday June 27

Columbus roads are one of the most beautiful I have seen in my travels around the world. The layout of most of the roads make them driver friendly and very safe to drive in if one follows the laws guiding operations of motor vehicles in Ohio State, the Buckeye State. They are very spacious and protective. Every lane is marked for different users. Some lanes are strictly dedicated for turning to the right or left while some are for driving straight only. A driver has enough space to change lanes if turning off to the right or left. The traffic lights are computed to pass vehicles sequentially without obstruction to all road users including pedestrians. Driving in Columbus is always a delight for a law abiding driver.

Monday June 27, 2011 Michael, Tolu and I arrived at the Bureau for Motor Vehicle, BMV office on West Broad Street, Columbus at about 9.30am. We entered the imposing glass building as the morning and warming breeze sun escorted the three of us in. The cool air conditioner inside the ground floor was just at the right roomy condition as we proceeded to the line at the reception. Three people were already ahead of us, a middle-aged man with a young man he was chatting with that looks like a teenager and an elderly woman that should be in her mid-sixties or more. Everyone has come for documentation or a license and either to assist someone else or for self.

To our right in the open hall are rows of long seats arranged in about eight seats each divided by aisles making about six rows that stretched towards the end of the hall. They all faced a stretch of counters with officials behind each calling and attending to customers. Computer cubicles separate the seating section from the end of the open hall.

"Next, please. Good morning. What can I do for you?" the female in blue uniform at the reception desk attended to us.

We are here for our temporary driver license," I responded.
Tolu and I came for our temporary driver license which will also serve as our identification cards for relevant and subsequent engagements.

"You can go to Counter 7," she pointed it out to us.

Over 60 people were seated in the hall waiting for their turns. Many more continued to come in, some like in a human convoy of six to seven people who have probably just arrived Columbus like us and need to have identification documents or driver license but needed interpreters, though the BMV has some in-house interpreters, especially in Spanish and Somali.

Some conclude their business on a counter while some are referred to another counter and to another counter. But business was always brisk as the officials seemed trained to attend to such a large crowd as brief as possible yet with required results.
Virtually all the desks have vision screening machines and some of the customers were asked to look into them to test their sight efficiency.

"Number 377, counter 7." The three of us got up and marched to the counter. I informed the lady that we came for our temporary driver license. She said the computer systems for the test were down and that we need to come back some other day. We requested for and got the the Ohio State identity card pending when we get the driver license. It cost Tolu and I about $50 to obtain.

Thursday June 30 we returned to the BMV office on West Broad for the driver license knowledge and vision test.
"Let me have your resident permit and social security cards, please." We handed over our passports which serve as our 'Green Cards' and the Social Security Number cards to the female officer across the counter. She gave us some forms to sign with markings on where to sign.

Because we were there for the temporary driver license we had to do the vision test before taking the knowledge test.

"Are you ready for the test?" We nodded in the affirmative.

Tolu and I had read the BMV booklet, **Digest of Ohio Motor Vehicle Laws**, in preparation for the test since it was given by a friend about 18days earlier. The booklet is free at all of the BMV offices. Tolu went first for the vision test and she read everything she was asked to read perfectly well. She was directed to computer number 13 to do her knowledge test.

The computer cubicles separating the seating section from the end of the open hall to the right were for the test. Every potential driver in Ohio State is required to sit for and pass the vision screening and knowledge test "to operate a motor vehicle on any public road, or any public or private property used by the public, for vehicular travel or parking."
There are about 30 questions and 75% is the pass limit. Any percentage lower than 75% at the end of the last question leads to a repeat of the test at another day. At least 24hours after.

I have been driving in Lagos, Nigeria for almost 20years yet I have to take the test which we don't do in Lagos but Tolu does not drive and so will have to learn how to drive the 'Columbus way'.

Tolu waited for me to also have my vision test and get my cubicle for the knowledge test assigned.

"Do you drive with your glasses on?" the lady asked me.

"Yes," I replied.

"Put your forehead on the black pad, look through the glasses and read the letters."

I was able to read the first line very well and managed the second line fairly well but could not read the rest of the remaining six or more lines.

"I am sorry I can't read further. They are very blurred," I informed her.

Even when she asked me to try again I could barely go into line three.

The examination for the glasses I was having on was done in Lagos over three years and I have not gone for another test.

The BMV lady filled a form, gave it to me and requested that I get new glasses and then come back for the vision test before I can sit for the knowledge test.

The result is that I failed the vision test and will have to repeat it.

'Wow!' What a way of discovering how weak one's eyes could be.'

It was surprising but better discovering it and fixing it than driving with blurred glasses that can not see far enough and be a danger to other road users.

Tolu went to Computer 13 and spent less than 20minutes. She passed the knowledge test and reported to another counter where the test is processed and other procedures for obtaining a temporary driver license are done. The officer in charge called her name, gave the temporary driver license to her to inspect for any error. And since there was no error, she was free to go!

The driver license cost about $27.

That evening I went to Walmart Store on Morse Road to book an appointment with an optician and got a Saturday July 2 at 11am.

On Thursday July 7, the glasses were ready and cost $106.

The BMV at West Broad was not opened on Saturday July 9 when I got there. Not all the BMV offices open on Saturday and so it is important to call the office before going or check online if they open on that day.

I returned to West Broad on Monday July 11 for my vision test which I scaled easily, this time, reading all the lines with ease from top to bottom. I was assigned my cubicle for the knowledge test.

Apart from reading the **Digest of Ohio Motor Vehicle Laws** handbook to prepare me for the knowledge test I did some test practice online on possible questions. Some of the contents of the handbook include Driver Licensing and Vehicle registration, Traffic Laws and Signs, Signals and Pavement markings.

Reading requires a lot of attention because the questions at the knowledge test have optional answers that in many ways may look similar but are actually different. If one fails to make 75% at the end of the 30 questions it becomes a 'fail' and must wait 24 hours before repeating the test. These are two sample test questions from the handbook:—

"A flashing red traffic signal at an intersection has the same requirements as which of the following?"

A. A slow sign
B. A yield sign
C. A stop sign
D. An intersection sign

2. When traveling on a highway divided into four traffic lanes, which vehicles are required to stop for a school bus that has stopped to unload children?

A. Only vehicles approaching the rear of the bus traveling in the same direction as the bus
B. All vehicles approaching the bus from either direction
C. No one is required to stop unless children are in view
D. All vehicles may pass the bus after providing an audible signal

The answers to the questions are C and A.

I got into the cubicle for my knowledge test. I did not need the ear phone which is placed there for those who cannot read with ease or require an interpreter in languages like Spanish or Arabic. A young man was already in the cubicle to my right busying away with his test while the cubicle to my left was empty. I was two more questions left when I received the congratulations sign. Otherwise it would have been 'sorry try again'.

My Ohio State Identity card was replaced with a Driver's temporary license referred to as **Temporary Instruction Permit Identification Card** (TIPIC).

I called on phone and got a Friday July 29 appointment for my **road and maneuverability test** at the West Broad Street office. It could also be booked online. Every **county** in Ohio State has one or more BMV offices but not all the offices carry out road and maneuverability test. BMV, West Broad, Columbus is under the Franklin County and a similar branch is at Cemetery Road, Halliard.

The maneuverability is done first where the driver is expected to drive forward through a box (9 feet by 20 feet) formed by four markers and drive back.

Prior to Friday July 29 two friends, Pastors Sanya Oyedola and Victor Oguntuyi helped me to improve on my driving skills especially the maneuverability skill which seemed tougher than the road test. I had bumped many times into the markers (cones) during practice and not parallel with test area.

"It is immediate failure running over or knocking down a marker, removing a marker completely from its designated area or other dangerous action."

An officer was assigned to supervise my driving that morning. He introduced himself and asked for my type of car and the tag (plate) number. A section of the parking lot at the West Broad office is dedicated to those who come for road test. He asked me to go into the car and directed I switch on the turning lights, the brake lights, and the wipers. After being satisfied, he opened the passenger door and sat beside me.

"You can back out and turn to the right," he said. I said some prayer inside me, did a good back out and turned to the right.

"Drive to where those markers are," pointing to the area. The area is dedicated to the maneuverability test. There is a test area beside it for motorcyclists.

"Drive through and turn to the left." I had prayed for that because I seemed to be better from the left angle, during my practice, than from the right angle. It was a good drive through and I stopped when he asked me to.

"Now back out,'" he instructed.

I moved slowly and steadily backward into the markers looking backward. I did not care to use the mirrors. I got in within the markers, straightened my hands and continued slowly praying in my heart not to knock down any of the markers.

"You can stop," he told me as the front of the car was almost parallel to the two markers at the start.

It was a heave of relief knowing that I passed the maneuverability test. People have lot of stories to tell of how they attempted the maneuverability test several times before they got their driver license.

"Drive through and turn to the right."

We headed to the West Broad road and into the opposite streets. The streets were quiet, not many cars apart from those parked on the sides. Even though I had the right of way, I slowed down at every junction.

"Why do you slow down at every junction?" he asked.

"In case another vehicle is coming in," I replied.

I observed every other road sign and felt good during the test. He directed me through until we were back to the BMV parking lot.

"You made nine stops at those junctions you were not supposed to. You have the right of way and should not have been stopping. You will need to do the road test again," he decreed.

Bad! I was confident I'd passed this one too. But my consolation was that I passed the maneuverability test and knowing that I failed the road test because of the stoppages at junctions.

My friend, Said Lawal, that took me in his car to the BMV office was waiting at the reception lounge to hear the result.

"You will pass it at the next try," he consoled me, after I explained what happened, as we walked out of the BMV imposing building.

I got Friday August 5 appointment for a repeat of the road test. This time, a lady officer was assigned to me. She went through the same process of introducing herself, asked my type of car, tag number, inspected the turning lights and brake lights.

"What happened at the last test?"

"I was told I stopped at junctions I was not supposed to stop. In Lagos, Nigeria where I am from, a driver needs to be very careful at such junctions because of other drivers coming out of those roads. That was why I was always slowing down at the junctions,' I explained to her.

She directed me into the same streets opposite the BMV building. After about 10 minutes of driving in the streets we were back to the West Broad BMV parking lot. "Congrats. You passed," she announced to me with a smile on her face.

It was 59days of living in Columbus, Ohio. I had estimated to have my full driver license two weeks of arriving the States.

It is very necessary that a family must have up to two cars to move around in Columbus, Ohio. And if there are teenagers in such a family that means additional car, especially, if anyone of them is a high school Junior or Senior. The public transportation does not cover every area. We live on Schrock Road, west of Cleveland Avenue, about 3minutes drive or 25minutes walk. The COTA buses ply Cleveland Avenue and do not come into Schrock Road.

It was therefore an urgent need for Tolu to have her driver license. She passed the maneuverability and road test same day in her second attempt on Thursday December 29. She did her test at the Hilliard BMV office. It was a great gift for a new year eve.

The conditions for teenagers from age 15 years plus half to obtain a driver license in Ohio are different from that of adult starting from 18 years and above and are all contained in the **Digest of Ohio Motor Vehicle Laws**. Every state in the United States of America has its own version of the Digest but the rules are almost similar. Every driver is expected to apply for a new driver license in a new state of residence.

According to the Digest of Ohio Motor Vehicle Laws, "if you are applying for a driver license before your 18th birthday, you must obtain either commercial or high school driver education consisting of 24 hours classroom instruction and eight hours of driving instruction. You should also provide a notarized affidavit signed by a parent or guardian verifying your completion of 50 hours of driving experience before taking the skills test. At least 10 of these hours must be night driving. A **driver education certificate** must be presented when taking the skills test."

Already 16 years old in September 2011, and with a temporary driver license Uyi began his high school driver education 24 hours classroom instruction on Monday February 20, 2012. It was conducted by an accredited driving school and lecture was at the Westerville Central High School. It cost $350 for the classroom instruction and the eight hours of driving instruction. These are in addition to the regular driving lessons supervised by Tolu and myself.

On Thursday March 1, the classroom instruction ended and Uyi scored 97 percent in the examination. He began the eight hours road driving instruction lesson on Monday March 12.

Wednesday May 23 Uyi was scheduled for his skill test (maneuverability and road test) at the BMV office, Hilliard. His desire is to get the driver license within the one year of use of the temporary license. Where he is unable to get the driver license within the one year he would have to resit and pass the knowledge test. That is the rule. Many teenagers do not wish to go through that experience twice. Only three people were on the line when it got to our turn.

We were almost 10 minutes late and wearied when we entered the office. Though, Uyi had preferred another county, Delaware for his skill test, I booked appointment for that of Hilliard. That is where he did his knowledge test and where Tolu did her maneuverability and road tests.

The male officer on the desk checked the list of those who booked and are expected for the day and the time.

"OMORUYI," he pronounced the full name.

"Can I have your driver education certificate?"

"I couldn't find it," he replied.

"You can not have your test without it. When you find it, give us a call for another appointment."

It was the reason why we were 10minutes late. We could not find the certificate and but decided we give it a try if possible they have it in their data base.

Uyi booked another appointment for Tuesday June 12, 2012. This time the appointment is at the BMV Delaware county on 2079 N. U.S Highway 23, Delaware. I picked him up from school, Westerville Central High School, at 2.30pm and we were at Delaware 10 minutes before scheduled time. I stayed behind why he left with the inspector so he doesn't get distracted seeing me watch. It was the same when Tolu did her test. I will rather wait for him to return and tell me the result.

The result is that he passed the maneuverability test and would need to repeat the road test for using a wrong lane. I was happy for him and know that he will be more cautious doing the road test next time.

Wednesday June 20, 2012 at 16 years, nine months and 14days, our son, Uyi passed his road test and became qualified motor vehicle driver. We marched gallantly to where we will formally request for the license. It was a relief for me. He can now drive himself to school and to work as he looked forward to working during the summer holiday.

The line to the counter was free.

"My son has just passed his test and we would like to have the license," I announced with some tinge of pride to the lady.

"Congrats!" she smiled at us.

"Let me have your Social Security Number card and resident permit," referring to Uyi "and your own driver license," referring to me.

Driver license is the official form of identification in many transactions. But we thought because Uyi has a temporary driver license that there was no need to bring along the Social Security Number card and resident permit.

"Wow! We didn't come with it."

"Sorry, we will need them to issue him the license," she said.

"You can get it from any BMV office close to you. You don't have to come here. It is already in the system," she added.

The next day we went to the BMV office at Westerville on N High Street, which is 5 minutes drive from where we live, to pick up the license.

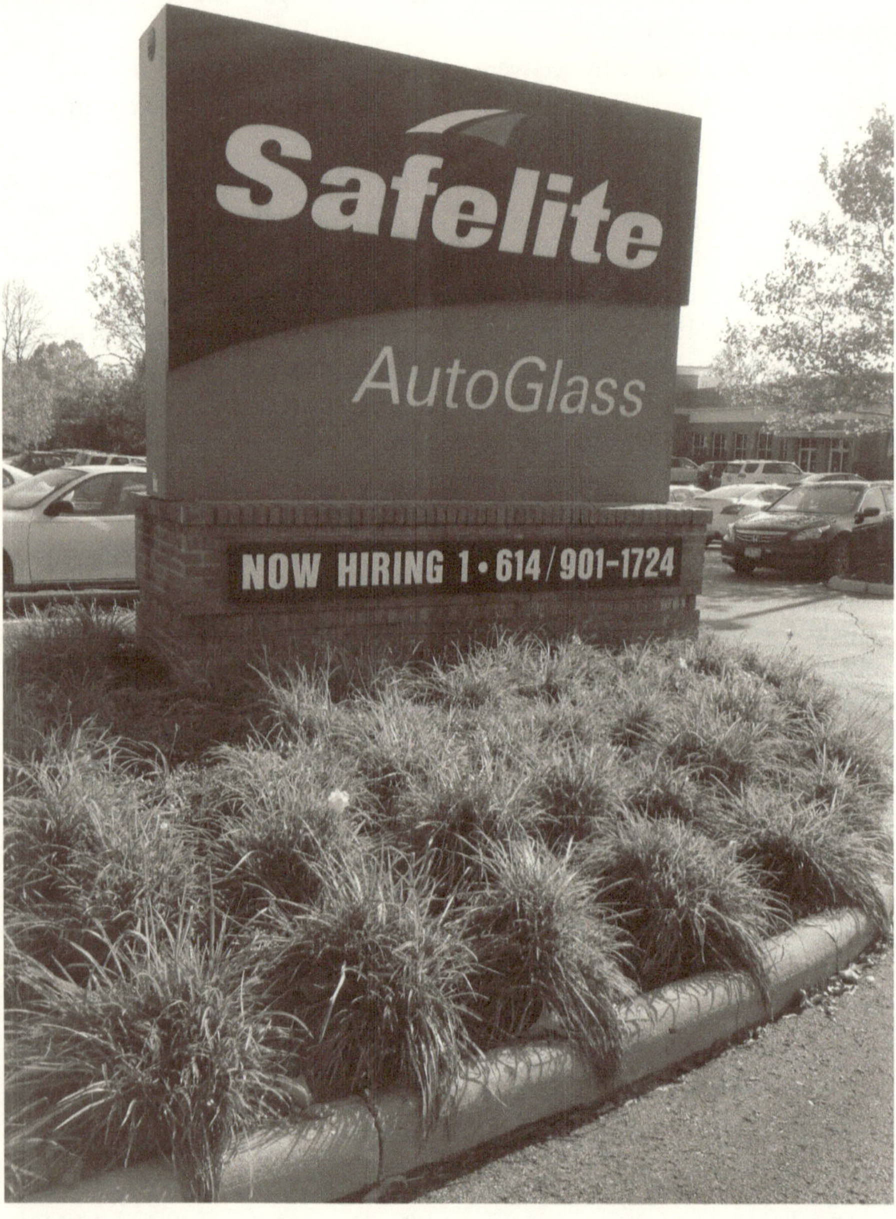
Safelite
AutoGlass
NOW HIRING 1 • 614/901-1724

Chapter 5

Job

Friday June 17

By the time we left Lagos, Nigeria for the United States on June 6, 2011, I had reduced the staff strength in my companies—Business Travel Publication; BT Tours and Airmedia Nigeria Company—to two from five within a period of five months, knowing that I would be away for a while. The operations are mostly aviation publications, aviation media consulting, travel management, promotions and events, including the Annual Lagos Airport Marathon.

We had worked for major Nigerian airlines like the Virgin Nigeria Airways, Aerocontractors Company of Nigeria, Dana Airlines, National Association of Nigerian Pilots and Engineers, National Association of Nigerian Travel Agencies and international airlines like the Turkish Airlines and Afriqiyah Airlines.

My main job goal in the United States was in the media, a job in a newspaper or magazine, in Columbus, Ohio. I went full course into applying online to as many newspapers in Columbus that I could access on the internet. I however, discovered that Columbus has only one daily general interest publication, the Columbus Dispatch, others are weekly and most are under the Columbus Dispatch Group; and also one business newspaper which I applied to work in but got a 'no vacancy' reply. I also applied to online publications that I was able to find.

On Friday June 17, 2011 I received an email from Examiner.com congratulating me that my application for a writer's job has been accepted and that I can start writing and publishing stories in their online publication. It was exciting getting this offer.

> "Dear Osadebamwen Uwadiae,
>   Your Examiner.com application has been accepted. Your Examiner title is the **Columbus Airlines Examiner** and you are currently an Examiner in the Columbus edition. Your channel, where your content will display on the site, is Travel.
>
>   Ready to get cracking? We're ready to help.
>   Congrats! You're officially on your way. We can't wait to see what you write!
>
> Thanks,
> Examiner.com

While waiting for our Social Security Numbers I had started looking online for possible jobs, journalism jobs especially. I remember discussing with Michael while still in Nigeria about the possibilities of getting a job as a journalist.

"That will be taken care of but the most important thing is arriving safely in the U.S," Michael had responded.

One of the job sites that attracted me while rummaging the internet for job was that of Examiner.com, a Denver, Colorado-based online publication. I was therefore very excited getting a reply from them requesting a write-up from me and later an acceptance of my application appointing me as Columbus Airlines Examiner for the Columbus edition of the magazine.

In a brief profile to Examiner.com, I introduced myself as a journalist since 1986 and major in aviation journalism since 1994 to date. Making me Columbus Airlines Examiner, therefore, was the most appropriate assignment for me being a familiar terrain.

I really never bothered about the remunerations at this time as I just needed to continue reporting which I had missed for 10days since we traveled from Lagos, Nigeria to Columbus, Ohio. But wages, according to the deal, would be paid based on some amount of cents to a certain number of visitors to the page or story. Therefore, getting this job 10days in the United States of America was the most encouraging this time. However, when it was time to process how I would be paid, I had to hold on because I was yet to receive my Social Security Number; it was requested for in the Paypal form for processing payment.

Work for Examiner.com started immediately. I visited the Port Columbus International Airport 24hours after the appointment as Columbus Airlines Examiner to see what it looks like, the offices and the airlines operating in and out of the airport. I contacted the media office of the Port Columbus International Airport, and introduced myself as Examiner.com Airlines Writer. My first work therefore came from a press release from the media office of Port Columbus International Airport and on Tuesday June 21, my first story was published on Examiner.com

"Port Columbus International Airport records 1.2 percent traffic

Osadebamwen Uwadiae
Columbus Airlines Examiner

Columbus, Ohio. June 20, 2011. Port Columbus International Airport, Ohio recorded 1,981,428 passengers in the first quarter of 2011 representing 1.2% growth of the same period last year.

Searches at the Columbus Regional Airport Authority show that there is a negative drop of 2.8% in total air mail of 948,970 and a negative drop of 7.9% in total air freight of 2,204,312 compared to same time in 2010.

A breakdown shows total 1,981,428 passengers in 2011 and 1,957,333 in 2010; air mail 948,970 in 2011 and 975,953 in 2010 with 2,204,312 air freight in 2011 and 2,394,649 air freight in 2011.

Nine airlines, AirTran, Air Canada Jazz, American, Continental, Delta, Frontier and Southwest, United and US Airways operate regular schedule flights to the airport. There are scheduled charters, non-scheduled charters operated as well in and out of the airport.

The nine regular airlines operating to the airport carried a breakdown of passengers of AirTran lifted 146, 580; air Canada Jazz 10,452; American 231,291; Continental 107,532; Delta 426,689; Frontier 31,449; Southwest 563,871; United 164,738; and US Airways 291,443."

I did several stories for Examiner.com between June and July 2011 mostly from the press releases sent to me by the Port Columbus International Airport. It was convenient just writing from the press releases at this time because of what it will cost going beyond that, by transporting myself to the airport or the airlines' offices. There was no earnings for me, though I recorded few visitors to the sites through my facebook friends.

The intensity to get a regular paying job intensified with the arrival of my social security number on June 24, 2011. My search mostly was media related—reporting, proofreading, and editing. Tolu's search was teaching and health services.

Days went into weeks and weeks into months. The only response was from Columbus First Business newspaper that there was no vacancy.

Tolu got an invitation for an interview at a courier firm located in Hilliard. On Thursday July 28, we were at the open interview together. There was a tour round the facility, also referred to as a *warehouse,* and we were shown the nature of the work. It was basically receiving and shipping. Packages from customers are received in bulk and they are shipped out for distribution. The sortings are done inside the warehouse. It was not the clerical office job we had looked forward to but still wanted it as we needed to work to afford accommodation and bring relief to our host and hostess who remained wonderfully encouraging keeping us in their home.

As we drove off from the warehouse in Hilliard to wait for employment letters our plan was on how Tolu will be on the second shift while I work the third shift. The employment letters or phone calls never came.

Within this period, however, several calls and emails for jobs in insurance companies had come which I never applied for. They probably got my contact through other job agencies that I also registered with online. The insurance companies were ready to train me but I will have to work based on commission.

"I need a regular paying job and not a commission-paying job," I explained to an insurance caller at a time.

Some of the job agencies we registered with included Monster, Simply Hired Alert, EmploymentGuide.com, Job.com Job Finder, Hoojobs and Beyond.com Alert. There are also signs of "Now Hiring" on display outside various companies, shops and warehouses that are hiring. I visit the library weekly to check job pages in the newspapers.

June 2011 grinds past. July came and was gone. August was around yet no paying job. Tolu and I visited a job agency on Schrock road where we met other job applicants. They were all busy filling out forms. I approached the lady on the other side of the counter.

"We will like to register with the agency for job," I said to her.

"Do you have warehouse job experience?"

"No!"

"The only recruitment we are doing now is for a warehouse job," the lady said. We left for home.

At home, Debra, Micheal's wife informed Tolu of a gourmet and gift company that was hiring seasonal workers and it was 15minutes drive from the house.
Seasonal jobs are jobs available and lasting the very season that the jobs are advertised. It could be for the summer, fall, winter or the spring season depending on the sales' expectation of the hiring company. They are most often in the warehouses.

There are a lot of activities that go on in warehouses with most being distribution centers for stores and online shoppers.

We were at the gourmet and gift company the next day, collected and filled application forms. Open interview was fixed for Tuesday August 2, 2011.
It was our first interview after the courier company's experience. Tolu went in first and came out after about 10minutes reporting that she has been offered a job. I went in next.

"Tell me about yourself," that was how the interview started. After a friendly chat that lasted about 10minutes I was hired. I was given a filled out paper to go for drug test at an address on Cleveland Avenue. Tolu also got the paper after her interview. The place was 5minutes' drive from the company and we went straight there to have our test. It was a urine test. Results are only sent to the company.

We both chose to work second shift which began 2.15pm to 11pm in order to take care of our kids' school or health demands in the morning. Also second shift pay was some cents higher than first shift at the company. Our pay was $8.75 per hour and we could work for between 35 to 40 hours a week.

The hours worked are based on demands by customers which, if low, the associates (workers) could be asked to go home at anytime and, if high, associates will work the complete hours or even work over time for whoever is interested. However, the joy of getting a paying job at last in the United States was more overwhelming than the figure of pay.

It means a new horizon opening on our path. A path to settling down, having a home, providing food in the house, paying electricity bill, gas bill, water rate, telephone and internet bill and putting gas in the vehicles. All these were becoming a reality as we drove home to celebrate a new dawn in our lives as new immigrants to the United States of America who are 'beginning life again' in the Columbus Way.

Orientation for the job was fixed for Thursday August 4. The Human Resources Manager welcomed the 12 of us at the reception hall that morning and invited us to the conference room. As we walked in line behind her through a passage, greeted by the fragrance of baked cookies, we could see a glimpse of what to expect through the glass opening on the white door leading to the kitchen, of associates (workers) in the morning shift. They all wore white aprons and net caps to cover their hairs and were busying away to meet expected time of production.

Parts of the orientation were a documentary of the job and safety procedures. Employment forms were filled and relevant information on deductions and taxes were documented. The HRM requested for the identification card (driver license or Ohio State identity card), social security number cards and resident work permit or a green card for non-citizen.

As we were leaving for home after the 2-hours of orientation which will be paid for, we already knew that the season could end in the last week of December 2011 or first two weeks of January 2012. However, some associates could be employed after the season if there are vacancies and based on performance.

Wednesday August 10 we received a call from the Human Resources Manager to formally resume work on Tuesday August 16, 2011. At 2pm, Tolu and I were there that Tuesday at the reception waiting to start work at 2.30pm. At about 2.23pm a man in white shirt and trousers with a white hairnet came and invited the five of us already seated at the reception waiting to begin work. He led us through the same passage that the HRM took us during the orientation.

As we approached the door to the kitchen, he stopped at the small piece of machine hanging on the wall.

"You will always clock-in here when you start work for the day, or when you go and you return from lunch break and when you close for the day," the man who we later knew as the shift manager informed us. He issued each person a clock-in card carrying number and names of owners. We clocked in.

He motioned to us towards a rack and asked that we put on white apron from a stack of aprons on the rack and the hairnets.

"Put on these any time you are going in," he said. Someone came out of the door to the kitchen and the shift manager held on to the door asking the five of us to go in. He took us to a spot and introduced the new seasonal workers to a lady, who we eventually knew to be the Seasonal Lead for the shift. She welcomed us while the manager left. "Watch what they are doing. That is what you will do for today,' she instructed. Associates were busy dropping cookies on to a conveyer that takes them into a chamber where they are wrapped and ready for public distribution.

'You go there," pointing to an open spot where someone in the morning shift was leaving. And the five of us were assigned to different spots to work on that day.

That point of our meeting where she did the assigning became the regular converging spot where we meet everyday to be assigned the day's job. Though we were offered to stay longer than the season which was to end in December 2011, we chose to seek other jobs and left in November.

The children were already on break in the summer of June 2012. Uyi, who has just completed his sophomore year in the High school, decided to experience how it is to have a holiday job. On Tuesday June 26 I took him round malls in and around Polaris Park Way to search for places that are hiring students for holiday job. He preferred to work in a place not too far away from school, where he can quickly get to after close of or end of sport's training at school. I encouraged him to do the seeking because he was already over 16years.

Job forms were filled at places and online but no offer seemed to be coming. Holiday was coming to an end as July closed; and Wednesday August 15 Uyi was back to school. But on Monday August 20 he already had two offers. He chose one and I went to his school to pick a Student Work Permit for him. It was an average of 12hours a week.

Chapter 6

Car

Saturday June 25, 2011

A car is a necessity in Columbus, Ohio. Public transportation does not reach most parts, especially for those living distance away from North Cleveland Avenue on the the north side.

And for a family of five that has two teenagers in the high school and one child in the elementary school it might just be right to have two cars to ease movement around the city.

Getting a car to buy in Columbus, Ohio is as easy as going to Walmart store to buy an item. Car dealers are everywhere. They are online as well, such as on the cars.com, autolist.com, autotrader.com, columbuscars. com; Craigslist and many others that can be searched for online. There are auction sales too such as at the Goodwill auction sale yard. It is advisable to have a company when going to buy from a Craigslist deal for safety reasons.

On our 17th day, Saturday June 25, 2011 in Columbus, Michael our host said we could buy a car. He has advised us before coming to America that we will need a car and that we should have a budget of between $2,500 and $3,500 for it.

"I have several dealers we can go to for a good car," Michael said.

"We will need a mini van because we are a large family," I told him.

Because Michael and Debra have a Honda Odyssey as their second car, we decided to go for a Honda Odyssey as well.

We found a 1999 model for $3,500 with 132,000 mileage from a car dealer on Westerville Road. It seemed a well used car with clean body, neat interior and good sounding engine. The dealer got the Title and temporary tag (plate number) for us from the Bureau of Motor Vehicle on Morse Road the same day.

On Thursday August 11, 2011, our friends, Grant and Iyore James gave us a second car, a 1997 Mercury Sable, to supplement the Honda and so we were saved the cost of buying a second car which was an inevitability as demands for the family movement around the city continued to soar.

The first maintenance challenge for the Honda Odyssey came on September 4. The account which was published on Pastor Bill's blog, the Pastor of Hillview Church, on East Main Street, Reynoldsburg, Columbus, is repeated here:—

"Sunday September 4, 2011 will forever be remembered by my family in the United States of America haven just arrived in June. We were on our way to our Church meeting at Blacklick Park, Reynoldsburg,Columbus, Ohio when our car broke down and I had to make it to the Hillview Church parking lot.

The first person that approached us wanting to know if we needed help was Pastor Bill Hayes. He helped to jump start the Honda Odyssey which responded a while but went off. Several members of the Church came to see what they could do while Pastor Bill called a Technician to come over and assist. We discovered that the Honda 1999 model Alternator was faulty and needed a replacement.

I gave a call to a brother in our own Church who came to pick me and another brother picked up my family while we went to get a new Alternator. Unfortunately, when we came back, the Technician had left for home and a call put through to him went into his Voice Mail.

I had already dispatched the brother that brought me as he needed to take his family home off North Cleveland Avenue before going to work.

As I was wondering what to do next, Pastor Bill came by and wanted to know how far with my arrangement. He also put a call to the Technician who could not be reached. He left, promising to get to the Technician through the parents.

Pastor Bill returned about 10minutes later changing into casual wears and announcing his clothes were wet because the Church just had a baptism that afternoon.

"We would have to fix the Alternator ourselves," Pastor Bill said.

He was with another young man, Ray Griffin. We started work on the removal of the Alternator and replacing it with the new one.

It started raining. In the rain we completed the work on the car, jump started it and alas, it was on and alive again. The rain was becoming heavy.

"Go into the car, and go and collect your money from Autozone for the recycling of the Alternator," Pastor Bill said. We bought the alternator from Autozone shop.

Where I come from, Lagos, Nigeria you don't fix your car yourself that way, especially replacing a Alternator. The mechanics fix it for you and you pay real big for it. So for me, it is a very big and an overwhelming deal doing it with Pastor Bill. To imagine a Pastor of a large Church, a parent and a grand parent, going to such a length to help is very humbling. He was an angel sent to us by God.

I actually drove from Wallcrest, Off North Cleveland Avenue to Reynoldsburg, a distance of over 30minutes. We are just three months in Columbus and missed our way with over six miles when we had the problem with the car. Everything that happened God knew and he used Pastor Bill to strengthen our own faith in his LOVE and we have resolved to be more giving and sacrificial, to the glory of His name."

The Honda was eventually sold on Monday November 12, 2012 when the transmission became faulty. Though the engine continued to work very well the transmission repair cost was between $1,500 and $3,500 at the time and because of our immediate finances and needs we opted for another car.

There are many car garages in Columbus where cars are serviced but for many months we were using home service for all our cars until it became unreliable and disappointing.

The last experience was when the radiator of the Mercury Sable became faulty; the mechanic started work on it and will not show up as promised any time appointment is fixed. When he eventually showed up, he did not put water in the radiator and ended up burning the gasket head. Unfortunately, we were not home when it happened and he never owned up or showed up to fix the problem and never apologized for what he did. We eventually junked the car for $400.

Fortunately, we found a garage on Hudson Street where the charges are affordable for repairs and had never used a home service since. Even when our car breaks down anywhere from home, we call a tow truck and it is taken to the garage. We have paid between $40 and $60 using such service. But for some, it is part of the insurance package for towing services.

We have continued to use Google map to find our way in and around Columbus. In the early days, we will print out the direction, but these days, knowing some of the land marks in the city, we just take down the nearest landmark and find our way.

There was a time we used the printed copy to a destination only to discover that it was the wrong place we printed out. When we called to know the right place, we could not afford to try because we were limited only to the direction in print. This could have been resolved with a navigator or a smart phone. Now we use both Google map and smart phone to find our ways in and around Columbus.

Chapter 7

Apartment

Tuesday August 2, 2011

Many apartments in Columbus offer appetizing incentives to potential tenants ranging from one month free rent to assurance of safe and secure apartments. It is common place to see signs such as "Free Rent" and "Now letting" in different apartments.

In the evening of Monday, June 20, 12days already in the City of Columbus, Ohio and while daily checking the mail box for our Social Security Numbers, my family and our hosts received some very *special visitors* led by the wife of a Nigerian Pastor, Amos Adetunji who leads one of the Nigerian community churches in the North side of Columbus. She had visited us a day after our arrival as she had knowledge of our coming. A very nice and pleasant woman from one of the states in the south west of Nigeria.

This time, she did not come alone but with a kind of entourage, two men, a lady and a little child of one of the men. It was indeed an *august visit* as they came with some food items for our host, on our behalf, as a support for accommodating us. It was a wonderful and very appreciative gesture from the *Yoruba church*, as we later learned to refer to it.

Their visit was also a time to know more about us, our plans for job, accommodation and our children's education. The visit was very informative and educative; and one of the men offered to assist in handling our accommodation after we must have settled down and started a job. He is Pastor Sanya Oyedola, "Pastor" as we call him.

"I will advise you live in Brookeville Apartments because of your children. It is a very good apartment to raise your kids,' Pastor Sanya said during the visit.

We became very close after the visit and he was one of two men that gave their time to help me with my car maneuverability practice before I went for my road and maneuverability test to obtain a driver license. He lived in Brookeville Apartments and desired we live there as well. The apartment was under the Westerville School District, meaning that our children in the High School will have option of attending Westerville South, Westerville North or Westerville Central High schools.

Fortunately, on Tuesday August 2, 2011 the day we went for job interview and employed at the gourmet company, also located in Westerville, we visited Pastor Sanya Oyedola to inform him so we can start the process for the accommodation.

He took us to the Brookeville Apartment Homes' office, sandwiched between a lawn tennis court and a swimming pool.

"Hallo!" the apartment manager, a lady welcomed us warmly.

"These are my brother and sister I spoke about. Hope we have vacant apartment? Pastor Sanya spoke as he introduced Tolu and I.

Application fee was $15 and we were registered and were put on wait list for a week so they could check our credit and rental history.

The Brookeville Apartment Homes comprises One Bedroom Garden (590 sq. ft for $510); Two Bedroom Garden (737 sq. ft. for $615), Two Bedroom Townhome (1127 sq. ft for between $715 and $765) and Three Bedroom Townhome (1485 sq. ft. for between $849 and $899). The accommodation manager requested we come with our pay stub when next we meet while they process our application.

On Tuesday August 9, we received a call from the Brookeville Apartment that our application was successful. However, we will need to wait till September 10, hopefully to move into the apartment that was being prepared for us.

On Wednesday September 7, 2011 Tolu and I signed a one year lease agreement. The next day we paid the rent and had to pay $650 security deposit which will be refunded when we decide to move out of the apartment and if there are no damages done to the apartment. The month's rent was based on pro-lateral, and the security deposit was because we were first time tenant in the US with no credit and rental history. We also paid the water rate.

Because the apartment can not share the electricity and gas bills equally like the water bill it is the apartment tenant's responsibility to deal directly with the two utility boards. I called the electricity and gas companies to let them know that we are now the new tenants of the apartment and payment and other documentations were done immediately on the phone.

It is very important and essential to have water running in the apartment together with electricity and gas, especially at this September when the early morning and late evenings were becoming too cold for new immigrants like us.

Saturday September 10, 2011, the keys to our apartment 1451 were ready and handed over to us. The beginning of the beginning!

Now with access to our apartment and home, on Friday September 16, we got a mobile phone line from H-2-0 ($40 unlimited calls monthly and $20 out of that $40 is for international calls so I can call outside America), a magic jack for the home (free calls through out the year within the US) and AT&T internet.

With the apartment taking shape gradually we eventually moved in on Sunday September 18, 2011. It was Day 103 on arrival to the United States of America.

Many kitchen and household items were donated to us by members of the Columbus Church of Christ where we worship.

That Sunday, September 18, my friend, Todd Hagar, saw a dryer and washer for sale on Craigslist for $50, and called me if he could buy them. He brought them to the house that night. These are heavy machines. Todd and his wife, Adrienne have remained sources of inspiration to my family ever since we arrived to the United States of America.

I have made efforts to keep a monthly record of regular spending in the house apart from food, mobile phones, gas for our three vehicles and other utilities.

November 2011		Total
Internet	$29.95	
Electricity	$14.81	
Gas	$67.44	
Water	$39.00	
Rent	$680.00	$831.00

January 2012		Total
Internet	$29.95	
Electricity	$93.28	
Gas	$98.51	
Water	$39.00	
Rent	$680.00	$940.74

April 2012		Total
Internet	$24.95	
Electricity	$118.00	
Gas	$39.22	
Water	$38.00	
Rent	$680.00	$940.74

- Note that the Gas went down as we did not need to use the heater this period (Summer) and the water rate slightly changed because of the change in the bill to the whole apartments which is shared according to each apartment.

August 2012		Total
Internet	$24.95	
Water	$35.00	
Gas	$33.11	
Electricity	$111.71	
Rent	$695.00	
Apartment Insurance	$120.00(Per Annum to an insurance company)	$1,019.77

- One year at the apartment—Note the increase in rent which has become annual and apartment's insurance which is also annual.

Chapter 8

School

Monday August 8, 2011

For a pretty large family with two kids already in High school and another one in elementary school the search for appropriate schools for them to attend in the neighborhood becomes a priority immediately the challenges of job and accommodation are taken care of. The kids must school in the district where they domicile with their parents or guardians. It has, therefore, always been our desire that Tolu and I are already working and the family settled down in our own apartment before the start of school.

Haven secured employment, though seasonal, and with an on-going processing of an apartment to live in, in the first week of August 2011, we took the three children to the Westerville City Schools Enrollment and Family Resource Center, located inside the OhioHealth Westerville Medical Campus along Polaris Park Way on Monday August 8 to process their school placement.

Being new immigrants we were informed at the Embassy in Lagos, Nigeria that the children will need to have a tuberculosis or TB test before being placed in schools. Other things we learned on arriving to the US were that we must live in the school district where we want the children to go to school with proof of residence in that district such as rent receipts, electricity and/or gas bills. The children will also be tested for the grades they would be or be placed in, which include for children with special needs. And if by any circumstance we move from a school district we were domiciling to another school district, then the children will have to change their schools to the new district of domicile. Changing schools in such circumstance does not pose any or much difficulties. What it requires are the same requirements as proof of rent or ownership, resident permit, electricity or gas bill and social security number.

The placement test was therefore fixed for the next Monday. Fortunately for the children there was a TB test exercise for students going to school in the neighborhood we were temporary staying which was fixed for the next day, Tuesday August 9. And that did it.

Thursday August 11 we received a call that the results of the TB test were ready for collection. They came out clean.

However on Friday August 12, we went to the Westerville City Schools Enrollment and Family Resource Center to submit proof of residence in Westerville school district and the children were with us. At the end of the documentation, the officer that attended to us advised that since the children were with us, they should have their placement test immediately. It was a big relief at the end of the exercise that the three of them passed their various grades' tests and were placed in schools. The teenagers were placed in the same high school and the 9-year old was placed in an elementary school closest to the apartment we live in.

There are basic things that must always be with a new immigrant which must be presented when processing things like this and they include resident permit, also known as the Green Card (could be in the international passport before the arrival of the Green Card); social security number card; contact address and phone number. These are very essential when going to places like the education board, Bureau for Motor Vehicle; new job and new registration at Children Hospital. The driver license serves for subsequent and other places.

Wednesday August 17, the children started school. Because it was their first day in a school in the United States, Tolu and I had to drop them off at school. The high school starts first, then the middle school and the elementary school. The buses that pick the students are scheduled to meet up within the time to pick students from designated spots.

First two days are not too smooth for the school bus drivers as students miss and mix buses to and from school. But as soon as this is fixed it is the most convenient means of getting the children to and from school for the children and parents.

At the Westerville Central High School, where Uyi and Abi were placed by the Westerville City Schools Enrollment and Family Resource Center we were already being expected at the school reception.

"How do you pronounce your name?" the lady asked Uyi.

We paid the school fees for the two of them amounting to about $80 for the year which was half of what we should have paid. We were considered new immigrants and barely two weeks on a job that pays $8.75 per hour. Uyi chose to start as a sophomore (10th grade) and Abi started as a freshman (9th grade).

At the Elementary school for Eki, the fee was about $15 for the year.

Thursday June 21, 2012 was a very hot day in the city of Columbus. Unfortunately, the aircondition in our apartment could not generate enough cooling effect to match the heat from the weather.
Columbus weather!

But it was my orientation day at the Ohio Center for Broadcasting situated at East Main street, Columbus. I had worked all my journalism life in the print media and also a graduate of Book Publishing from the Yaba College of Technology, Lagos. Therefore, haven spent almost one year in Columbus without a job in that particular media sector I agreed with my former airport correspondent colleague in Nigeria, now based in Columbus, to go back to school and explore opportunities in the electronic media.

Incidentally, the school runs a one-year Diploma program which was very convenient and right for me to add to the broadcasting knowledge that I had at the Nigerian Institute of Journalism, Lagos between 1983 and 1985.

About 22 of us were at the school for the orientation. The school's aircondition was perfectly set to match the weather. After introduction and briefs by the education director, we were taken round the school facilities—television studio, editing bay, radio and production studios, the school radio station and the computer laboratory used for website management and design lectures.

The education system made my return to school seamless. I had visited the school earlier and was formally invited to a facility tour. At the end of which I filled out the necessary forms for admission and my class was the June Day Class of 2013. The school has facilities for grants and education loan which I got. I received the federal government grant of $5,000 and another $550. I did an exit counselling of the loan days before graduation where I learned how, when and what to be paying back at six months after graduation.

My classes were on Monday, Wednesday and Thursday 9am to 1pm. I never missed a day. Though my "late times" amounted to several days, because I had to wait for the school bus to pick my daughter to her elementary school at 8.30am. And I had to make the 30minutes journey to school.

Most times I am right on dot at school but other times, I get to school at 9.05am and the accumulation of these minutes amounted to days which I made up for with extra laboratory hours at the radio and television studios.

At graduation on Thursday June 13, 2013, the class that started with 22 students thinned down to 12 students. But the one year was a unique and wonderful experience for me learning from experienced on-air talents, program and production directors in radio and television that come regularly to the school to share their experiences with students. The school days fit perfectly well with my weekend job. It also fits with the second shift that I work, especially if I need to work Monday or Thursday. I could attend classes without it affecting my job and fortunately the school was located 10minutes away from where I work.

Chapter 9

House

Thursday January 24, 2013

When we moved into our apartment in September 2011 the rent was $650. The contract was for one year and was renewable. Two months before the expiration of the contract we got a notice for renewal. We signed all the necessary documents for renewal and when it was time to pay the rent it went up to $695.

Now that we prefer a month-by-month pay the rent moved up to $765. We chose the month-by-month option because we only need a one month notice without paying in lieu of the one month before moving out of the apartment because we decided to buy a house.

In a six-months or a one year contract we will pay a month rent in addition to the one month notice which we do not have to pay in a month-by-month option.

I was at our bank on Thursday January 24, 2013 when I saw a notice of a Mortgage Workshop. I thought to myself that it will be fine to have the bank finance our mortgage. But there are many mortgage finance houses that one is at liberty to use. Though I did not make the workshop which was that weekend, I met the Mortgage Officer formally on Friday February 1.

"Good to meet you," the mortgage officer said, as I entered his office cubicle, directing me to a seat opposite his.

"Let me know the kind of house you want, the district and the monthly payment you can make conveniently,' he requested.

"A four-bedroom house, in Westerville School District. Our children attend schools in the district and we do not want to change their schools at the moment. We can pay a rate not too higher than what we pay as rent presently" I responded.

"I will need your resident permit, social security card, pay stubs and tax returns for 2011 and 2012 to see what mortgage you're qualified for. This will enable us prepare a pre-approval for you," he informed.

The mortgage officer also wanted to know if we have a realtor already. We did not have one. He arranged a meeting with a realtor who I met on Saturday February 9.

Work started with the realtor officially on Monday February 11, 2013 when he took Tolu and I to inspect two houses. The houses were both four-bedrooms, good prices within our range, but they only have one full bathroom each.

"We want a house with two full bathrooms, one must be in the master-bedroom," I said to him.

We inspected another house on Saturday March 2. The house looks nice from the outside. But as we huddled through the freezing cold outside that evening into the living room of the house, the realtor said, "We can't take this one. It has plenty signs of mold around," pointing to dark stretches of marks on the walls.

On Friday March 8, we found a beautiful house that met our taste. Many people seemed to be interested in the house too based on the number of visitors who signed the house inspection's list placed on the kitchen table. We made our first bid for a house that evening when the realtor sent an electronic version of the offer papers to my mail box. The result came seven days later. Our bid fell through. Our bid was beaten by someone who made a higher bid.

We continued to inspect more houses and may have inspected close to 15 houses when on Thursday May 23 we found another interesting house that was right for our taste and budget. We made our offer, this time with $10,000.00 above our budget.

On Wednesday May 29 our realtor called me to announce that our offer has been accepted. It was a celebration at home that at last we will have our own house. But it is only the beginning of another exercise, the real part of buying a house, and that is the approval of the loan or mortgage by the financing firm.

It is for one to find a house to buy it is another for the mortgage financing firm to accept to finance the house, even where the mortgage officer would have been very encouraging. So many things are involved and could some times be frustrating.

On Friday May 31 I was at the house with a property inspector introduced to me by the realtor. He inspected every part of the house, the structure, equipment and electrical connections. We paid him $300 for the inspection. I received the Inspector's report on Sunday June 2—a 15-page report with photographs of immediate and future repairs in the house. The repairs were pretty much and could cost over $15,000 to fix all while the immediate repairs could cost about $7,000.

The realtor and I met with the Mortgage officer on Monday June 3 and went through offer and approval papers, and the inspector's report.

"We will need to wait for the bank's appraisal of the house," he said and we fixed another meeting for Friday June 7 for Tolu and I to sign more papers.

Friday June 7, 2013 made it two years that we immigrated to the United States of America. At 10am we were waiting for the Mortgage officer at the bank. He came in about 15minutes. The paper works were much as we went through and signed virtually all the pages of the 30-page documents.

"How long have you been in the US?" the Mortgage officer asked. "Two years today," I replied. "I've asked the question before and I am asking again for formal documentation" he explained.

"Three deposits were made into your account, why?" The question took us by surprise. "It's our money and I deposited it," I replied.

"Yes, we will like to know so that it doesn't seem money is quickly paid into the account for the Mortgage approval or some illegal deposit."

We are used to having cash at home. When the salaries go into the account, we withdraw the amount of cash we would like to spend at home; something we've been doing from Nigeria.

But it is not necessary in America to keep cash at home. Most businesses can be transacted with the debit or credit card. Our experience in our part of the world has taught us not to always leave everything at the bank, despite the high risk of having cash at home. However, it is very safe in our new environment to leave the money in the bank because it is actually secured, insured and assured.

I wrote a memo explaining the three deposits into my account. We completed all the signings, shook hands and looked forward to a final approval by the bank's mortgage department.

Thursday June 27 we received two bulky white envelops from the bank. I did not bother to open it because we had received such parcels earlier which contained the over 50 pages of work paper we read and signed with the Mortgage officer. He had called at the time for Tolu to come to the bank and sign additional documents which were not signed at the last meeting.

On Saturday June 29, 2013 morning I decided to open one of the envelops. The first page was headlined "Statement of Credit Denial, Termination or Change". I followed other subtitles like the "Description of Account, Transaction or Requested Credit" which in our case is "FHA-Fixed Rate" and below it was "Description of Action Taken".

I did not see the action taken even though it was written immediately under it but was attracted by the white bold words on black which read "Principal Reasons for Credit Denial, Termination or Other Action Taken Concerning Credit".

Arranged in two equal tables, right and left, were 34 check lists of reasons for credit denial, termination or other action taken concerning credit. I ran my eyes through the list and every box looked unchecked. I went through it again carefully wanting to be sure, but there was a check mark on box 7 which was "Length of Employment".

The meaning is that we are denied the credit based on our length of employment in the United States of America. The denial was a big blow. "7" was supposed to be a very lucky number for us but this time it is a denial for what should be our first house in the US. Tolu and the children were disappointed. A lot of planning had been going on on who should be in what room and what must be done to keep the house always clean and attractive.

However, we were consoled by the fact that the refusal was based on length of employment and not other difficult grounds. We started work in August of 2011 and two years of employment will be August 2013.

For me, it was a relief from the work and repairs that we would have been compelled to carry out in the house before moving in.

The probable grounds for refusal could include but not limited to Credit Application incomplete; Insufficient Number of Credit References Provided; Unacceptable Type of Credit References Provided; Unable to Verify Credit References; Temporary or Irregular Employment; Income Insufficient for Amount of Credit Requested and Excessive Obligation in Relations to Income.

Other grounds are Unable to Verify Income; Length of Residence; Temporary residence; Delinquent Past or Present credit obligation with others; Collection Action or Judgment; Garnishment or Attachment; Foreclosure or Repossession and Bankruptcy.

Also included are Number of Recent Inquiries on credit Bureau Report; Value or Type of Collateral not sufficient; Unable to Verify Residence; No Credit File; Limited Credit Experience and Poor Credit Performance with the mortgage firm.

If we had known some of these conditions, we probably would not have started the process but would have waited for the right time. The mortgage officer had assumed everything was right until the refusal came.

On Friday August 23, 2013 I met with the mortgage officer to resume from where we stopped.

After a meeting with our Mortgage officer, we decided to take time off the search for a house. The Mortgage firm was dropped. The time off was for almost eight months. But it was worth it because we got a new realtor, Tayo Oladele of Royal Executives Realty.

On Tuesday April 22, 2014 I received a first call from our new realtor to inspect a house at Gray's Market Drive. It was a beautiful four-bedroom house with two and a half baths. We made a bid on Wednesday April 23. On May 6 we learned that our bid was not adequate enough.

When we made another bid for a house on Serene Place, Off Cleveland Avenue on May 16, we were confident that it will be ours because of the offer we made. But the next day, we learned that the house has gone into multiple offers and we may need to increase our initial offer. However on Thursday May 22 the news was that our bid fell through again. Now we are getting used to making bids!

Interestingly on the same day Thursday May 22, our resilient realtor invited me to inspect another house at Gravenhurst Court. The house looks small from the outside but became the biggest house we ever inspected. It was placed in the market same day by a bank. The last two houses that our bids failed were put on sale by the owners.

After inspecting the ready to move-in house at around 1pm, I immediately mandated our realtor to put in our offer that day.

Seven days after we made an offer, Thursday May 29 the news was 'successful". It was The House! All other misses and failings for a house were a pathway to this house. Our Mortgage officer at Loan One was excited and ready to commence with the processing. I was asked to do the Homeowners' Guide exam online. I read and passed after two weeks.

The appraisal was done. It cost $300. The result of the appraisal was that the real market value of the house was $18,000 less than the bid we made. The bank was magnanimous enough to waive the difference which we would have been compelled to pay.

The mortgage officer in liaison with our realtor continued the processing, demanding for required documents to close the deal. We paid $1,000 earnest money, which is a deposit to assure the owner/seller that we are serious about buying the house. The amount is added to whatever amount that is expected to be paid as closing cost.

Friday July 11, the deal was closed with all documents signed. We went to the house and changed the locks.

Friday July 18, 2014 we moved into our house. It was three years, one month and 11days after touching down at the O 'Hare International Airport, Chicago, Illinois and three years, one month and 10 days in Columbus, Ohio as immigrants from Lagos, Nigeria, West Africa.

Chapter 10

Citizenship

Thursday, July 21, 2016

'As they were shouting and throwing off their cloaks and flinging dust into the air, the commander ordered that Paul be taken into the barracks. He directed that he be flogged and interrogated in order to find out why the people were shouting at him like this. As they stretched him out to flog him, Paul said to the centurion standing there, "Is it legal for you to flog a Roman citizen who hasn't even been found guilty?"

When the centurion heard this, he went to the commander and reported it. "What are you going to do?" he asked. "This man is a Roman citizen."

The commander went to Paul and asked, "Tell me, are you a Roman citizen?"
"Yes, I am," he answered.

Then the commander said, "I had to pay a lot of money for my citizenship."
"But I was born a citizen," Paul replied.

Those who were about to interrogate him withdrew immediately. The commander himself was alarmed when he realized that he had put Paul, a Roman citizen, in chains'. (Acts 22: 23 – 29 Holy Bible – New International Version)

American! An American is a citizen of the United States of America. There is something unique about this tag "American" – it is that pervading aura of pride with a sense of security that comes with the consciousness of regarding oneself as a citizen of "God's own country."

The very first time this tag rang a bell in my ears was sometime in 1993 while covering an assignment, as an aviation reporter, at the Murtala Muhammad International Airport, Lagos, Nigeria. There was this man, very sure was a Nigerian, who had some issues with airport officials at one of the check-in counters.

As the situation became escalated, the man blurted out, "I'm an American!" Everyone around suddenly stopped and turned to see who this "American" was. It worked for the man because he was eventually treated nicely and with much respect.

Being citizens of some countries confer so much admiration, adoration, honor and respect just like Paul was eventually treated by the Roman Army Commander in the Holy Bible (Acts 22: 22-29).

However, it is important to note that even though Paul was in chains, he was not deterred to speak out about his citizenship, knowing with confidence, the rights and responsibilities of a citizen. It helped him out of trouble.

To be chained is being restricted from performing or denied free movement. An unchained person has the freedom to perform and move freely.

Some of the reasons for which the colonists came to America in the early times included freedom, political liberty, religious freedom, economic opportunity, and escape from persecution.

According to "Learn About the United States: Quick Civic Lessons for the Naturalization Test", "In the 1600s and 1700s, colonists from England and other European countries sailed across the Atlantic Ocean to the American colonies. Some left Europe to escape religious restrictions, to practice their religion freely. Many came for political freedom, and some came for economic opportunity. These freedoms and opportunities often did not exist in the colonists' home countries. For these settlers, the American colonies were a chance for freedom and a new life.

Today, many people come to the United States for the same reasons."

Coming to America in June 2011 on the Diversity Visa Program, also known as the US Visa lottery, was in line with some of the reasons the colonists came – "freedoms and opportunities" with new life. We were also aware of the opportunity of becoming citizens of the United States of America within certain period, provided we remain responsible and law abiding residents during the required time.

In the morning of Monday, March 7, 2016, four years and nine months after we immigrated to the United States, I went to the Post Office located at the corner of Cleveland Avenue and Dublin-Granville Road, in Columbus, Ohio to post the N-400, Applications for Citizenship for four out of five members of the family – myself, Tolu, with the children, Abi and Uyi (18 and 20years old). The third child, Eki, as a minor at 13-years old, will be covered by the status of the parents.

I had downloaded the N-400 forms online and printed them out in February. The cost per person at the time of application, $680, which if broken down included $595 naturalization filing fee and $85 for biometrics services.

"You can track it online to confirm delivery by latest 03/14/16," the associate at the Post Office said, handing over to me the half torn green form used in documenting the items in the parcel with the expected date of delivery written in pink ink.

Monday, March 14 we received letters from the United States Citizenship and Immigration Services, USCIS acknowledging that our applications have been received on March 9, 2016 and in process.

A second Notice of Action came on Saturday, March 26 requesting that we should go for biometrics and have our fingerprints taken at the Application Support Center on Westerville Road on Tuesday, April 5 at 8am. A distance of less than 10minutes drive from home.

Westerville Road, Columbus is a continuation of the Westerville Uptown State Road crisscrossing Schrock Road, Dublin Granville Road, Morse Road and ending on south end of Cleveland Avenue. The Application Support Center could be found in a building of offices and shops at Alum Creek Plaza behind AutoZone.

Two vehicles were already parked opposite the Support Center when we arrived few minutes before 8 o'clock. Office was not formally opened but the lights inside were on. The four of us were at the entrance when the door opened.

"Good morning." I gave the four notification letters to the officer at the front desk. She passed out four Applicant Information Worksheets to be filled. Each person was issued a number.

"Go to any of the desks that calls your number," she informed.

Two desks were operating that morning. The exercise was simple, a brief of what to do, finger prints, and a photo. Each person spent an average of 10minutes. We were done within 25minutes.

"The book in this package contains the questions and answers you will be asked during the citizenship interview. Read it and you can listen to the CD as well. Everything in the book is in the CD," the officer explained.

The book in the package has a title, **"Learn about the United States: Quick Civic Lessons for the Naturalization Test"** with a CD, inserted in a bag attached to the last page. The 31-page book helps applicants study for the civics and English portions of the naturalization interview. It has 100 civics (history and government) questions on the naturalization test.

According to the introduction, "Applicants who are 65 or older and have been a permanent resident for at least 20years at the time of filing the Form N-400, Application for Naturalization, are only required to study 20 of the 100 civic test questions for the naturalization test. These questions are flagged with an asterisk (*)."

Though we were not sure when the interview letters will be sent, we all read the book, at least twice. Very often, we listened to the CD while in the car.

It starts with **"What is the Supreme law of the land?"**

"The Constitution," the answer.

On Saturday, May 14, 40days after the Biometrics, we received four letters of Notice of Action requesting that we appear for Naturalization Initial Interview at the LeVeque Tower, 50 West Broad Street, in downtown

Columbus on Thursday, June 16, 2016. Each of us scheduled for different time, but within two hours.

"You are hereby notified to appear for an interview on your Application for Naturalization at the date, time, and place indicated," according to the letter.

Parking space is always a challenge in downtown Columbus. Parking space rate is from $5 to $20 depending on the park owners, time and location, but locating one could be stressful.

One may be fortunate to get the meter park on the streets for as little as $1.75 for two hours. This is rare during office period and risky if one exceeded the time paid for. The fine is as high as $75.

We searched out for a parking space close to the interview venue a week before the day. The parking space attached to the building, which is on 40 N Front Street, has seven levels. All spaces on the first four floors are reserved for offices and staffs of different organizations in the building. It can exacerbate a first time visitor who is unaware of the reserved spaces and may result to being late for appointment.

On the average, the interview time was 15minutes for each person. Two examiners were on duty during our schedules. They interviewed one at a time.

The same examiner interviewed Tolu and Uyi, our son while the same examiner interviewed Abi, our daughter and I.

I was the last to be interviewed.

"Your daughter did very well during the interview," the examiner informed me.

"I hope you will do well too."

He briefed me on what we will be doing and the number of questions.

"If you answer the first six questions correctly, then we are done."

I was asked the basic questions on personal conduct and responsibilities, including up to date payment of taxes.

"Write down on this paper 'The capital of Ohio State is Columbus.'"

The questions I was asked included the Supreme Law of the land; governor of Ohio State and the parts of the U. S Congress.

I answered the first six questions correctly.

"You passed!" my examiner announced. He issued me the Naturalization Interview Results.

The examiner has options of two decisions 'A' and 'B'. The 'A' option reads "Congratulations! Your application is recommended for approval. At this time, it appears that you have established your eligibility for naturalization. If final approval is granted, you will be notified when and where to report for the Oath Ceremony."

The 'B' option reads "A decision cannot yet be made about your application."

One week after the interview, Thursday, June 23 we received notification letters for Naturalization Ceremony scheduled for Thursday, July 21, 2016 at the U. S. District Court Southern District, 85 Marconi Boulevard, Columbus, OH 43215. U. S. District Court, None.

Few days before the ceremony, I went with Uyi to search out Marconi Boulevard. It was the next parallel street to N Front Street, the location of the car park used by visitors to 50 West Broad Street, the interview place. It is linked by W Gay Street to the car park.

Officials are very strict with dress code for the ceremony. A reminder note issued for the ceremony specifically stressed the need to put on proper attire.

"Proper attire should be worn. No jeans or jean skirts, shorts, tennis shoes or flip flops," the note warned.

"Please arrive promptly at 8.15am to prepare for the final interview at 8.30am. The Oath Ceremony will begin at 10.00am."

"Attention: If you arrive late you will not be naturalized!" it added at the bottom of the letter.

Citizenship Oath Ceremony

We arrived the venue of the Oath Ceremony at the U. S. District Court Southern District, 85 Marconi Boulevard, Columbus, OH 43215 on Thursday, July 21, 2016 before 8am. Though Uyi and I spent much time looking for a space to park at 50 West Broad Street parking lot, where we had to drive to the topmost floor, we entered the venue before the commencement of ceremony.

The passage to the event room was already teeming with participants and guests, all adorning beautiful clothes, with some in the Star - Spangled Banner colors of red, blue and white. It oozed with the ambience of celebration!

"Good morning and welcome to Citizenship Oath Ceremony," the coordinator, Ms Fran Green, formally welcomed the "new Americans" and guests at about 8.30am. She explained all that will be done for the day.

"No jeans, or jeans skirts, shorts, tennis shoes or flip flops," she reiterated.

"Seats have been reserved in the room for only participants for the first session. Guests will be invited in for the final event."

Fifty five participants were candidates for the Citizenship Oath Ceremony from 26 countries, with some of the countries being Nigeria, Sierra Leone, Ghana, Ethiopia, Somalia, Britain, Ireland, Poland, Netherlands, Chile, Mexico and Dominican Republic.

A video was played of President Barack Obama welcoming and congratulating the new Citizens of the United States.

All documents including Permanent Resident Card ("green card"); All Reentry Permits or refugee Travel Documents, valid or expired; and any other documents that the United States Citizenship and Immigration Services, USCIS issued were returned during the first session.

Everyone received the voters' registration form at the end of the first session.

"Fill and return the voters' registration forms when you come back for the next session," the coordinator said.

This conveyed a feeling of the new inclusiveness as an American citizen eager to fulfil one of the inalienable rights by participating in the 2016 Presidential Elections scheduled for Tuesday, November 8. There is no best time as this as becoming a Citizen of the United States and a deciding factor in the general elections.

About 15minutes after the interlude, everyone returned and submitted the voters' registration form.

"The next event, which is the Oath Ceremony will take place in the Court room before the Judge. Family members will be allowed in to witness it and pictures are allowed," the coordinator informed as we listened in anticipation.

The courtroom was set, except for the Judge as the 55 participants took their seats. Guests were ushered in to fill the remaining empty seats.
We all rose as Ms. Fran announced the arrival of the Judge.

"Sit down please," Magistrate Judge Terence P. Kemp said with a gesture, smiling as he surveyed the court room.

Proceedings began promptly as every participant made a brief but almost similar introduction.

"My name is Osadebamwen Uwadiae. I am from Nigeria and I am happy to be a citizen of the United States." All the participants introduced themselves using almost the same line.

Congratulations! You are now Citizens of the United States of America" Magistrate Judge Terence P. Kemp announced at the end of the Oath Ceremony.

This came exactly on the 1,822nd day of arriving the O'Hare International Airport, Chicago, Illinois State.

Everyone had a privilege of a hand shake and picture with the Judge.

My friend, Todd Hagar and the Evangelist of the Columbus Church of Christ, Bob Shanks were our guests and they also joined in the photo session.

At the conclusion of the ceremony and as we walked down the stairs outside of the Court House on 85 Marconi Boulevard, with the glowing sun shimmering down on our beautiful attires, the passing cars and all the tall buildings around standing erect like mounting a guard of honor, it dawned on me that it's been 1822 days in the United States of America.

We had entered the Court House building that morning of July 21, 2016 as resident green card holders in the United States, and two and a half hours later, we stepped out of the building as Citizens of the United States of America.

Every step we took down the stairs of the Court House towards the road as we headed to the car park on N Front Street, was an "American Step".

Now I understand why the man at the Lagos airport, years ago, was proud to say "I am an American". American… Yes, I am!

www.ingramcontent.com/pod-product-compliance
Lightning Source LLC
Chambersburg PA
CBHW050431290526
45786CB00003B/1489